Greenwood

Let's Go Metal Detecting

Everything you need to know to get out in
the field this weekend

Please return when finished

Table of Contents

Intro

Firstly, thank you for purchasing this book, I am truly grateful.

There are plenty of books out there on the hobby of metal detecting. What this book is intended to do is speed up your learning curve and get you out there enjoying the hobby as quickly as possible. I've spent years in the hobby, learning from other hobbyists and from my own experiences in the field. It is my intention to help you improve your skills and finds by passing on to you what I've learned from my time in the field.

One thing you won't find here is technical data on how machines operate. This is primarily because I'm not a techie but also because I don't see it as necessary. I don't know how a smartphone actually works, but I can still use one effectively anyway.

If you've already got the basics down, worry not. There is information in here for the experienced detectorist as well. I've spent countless hours swinging a metal detector over the last twenty plus years and have learned many lessons along the way. These lessons I will share with you within these pages.

Before we get started, it is important to understand that you are the face of the hobby.

What you do, and how you represent the hobby, is how many people will view the hobby.

When out in the field, assume that you are being watched because it's likely that you are. It is your job to protect the hobby by presenting a positive image and behaving appropriately.

With this in mind, below is my condensed version of the metal detectorist's code of ethics:

1. **Fill all holes, take all trash.**
2. **Be respectful of others and courteous at all times.**
3. **Work to leave no trace of your presence wherever you metal detect.**
4. **Do not alter or move any plants, structures, signs, or other objects when you are out in the field.**
5. **Respect private property and never metal detect private land without the permission of the rightful owner.**

Equipment

Before you go out and drop a small fortune on equipment, I'll do my best to give you the low-down on what you really need to get started in the hobby as economically as possible.

Most obviously, you need a detector. These days, entry level models from major manufacturers are really good, and there isn't a need to buy a sophisticated one until or unless you really know you'll stick with the hobby. I'd recommend any of the entry level machines from Fisher, Garrett, Whites, or the Go Find series of detectors from Minelab. All can be had for $250 or less. There are plenty of other manufacturers out there, but these are the models I have personal experience with, and I won't recommend a product I haven't personally evaluated. If you feel that an entry level machine just isn't for you, then you can't go wrong with any of the Garrett AT series machines. At around $500, you'll get a very good and versatile machine for your money and you won't soon outgrow it.

You'll need a digging tool obviously. This can be the garden trowel you likely already have in your shed. If not, you can buy one for $5 at your local hardware store. If you have to have the real deal, get a digger from Garrett, Lesche, or Whites. By "digger" I mean a small, handheld tool with a serrated edge designed for planting flowers. A shovel is a different tool altogether.

A pouch is absolutely necessary, and all you really need is a $1 apron from your hardware store. You'll have a pocket for your keepers and a pocket for your trash. If you really want to, go ahead and spend $10–$40 on a pouch from any of the major detector manufacturers or whatever you want on a carpenter's belt, the sky's the limit there.

You will absolutely need a pinpointer. This is the small, handheld detector about the size of a large carrot you probe the ground with to pinpoint the exact location of your target. It will save you both time and frustration in locating targets in the ground and will give you more time for searching as you spend less time locating your find.

Pinpointers are worth every penny and this is not the place to cut costs. I highly recommend the Garrett Pro Pointer AT, the so-called "Garret Carrot", or if you've bought a Garrett machine, get the Pro Pointer AT Z-link, which communicates wirelessly with your headphones. The Garrett Pro Pointer II is a good pinpointer, but for only a few dollars more the AT is a significantly better option due to being waterproof and having three levels of sensitivity. I've also had success with the Vibraprobe series of pinpointers, they and the AT are waterproof and you can't go wrong with either one.

Everything else you will need to start in the hobby can be very basic, and should you find the hobby is for you, you can always upgrade when your skill level outgrows the capabilities of your equipment.

Believe it or not, you will need a pair of headphones. They block out ambient noise and help you hear faint signals. To start with, any pair of headphones will do—literally any pair. Chances are you have one lying around the house somewhere. If you decide the hobby is for you then I'd recommend the Garrett Z Link MS-3 wireless headphones. They are comfortable and invaluable in the amount of time they save you by not having to fiddle with a cord every time you get down to recover a target. This system works with any detector, not just Garrett machines. An unintended bonus of a full-sized set of headphones is that your ears don't get sunburnt in the summer and they protect you from cold and wind in the winter.

That is all you need to get started, and if you're casual about the hobby, it's all you'll ever need. Less than $400 is all it takes to get started in the hobby. If the fever really grabs you, you will have plenty of opportunities to upgrade your equipment down the road.

Other things to consider are a pair of kneepads for obvious reasons; though I've never used them, some people do. Two-way radios can be very helpful in the woods or on large properties when you want to communicate with a hunting partner.

Choosing your detector

Choosing the right detector can be a daunting task; there are many manufacturers, each with multiple models, so how do you choose?

There are a number of questions to ask before purchasing.

1. What's your budget?
2. What type of detecting do you envision doing (parks, fields, woods, beaches)?
3. Are you a techie and want to be able to choose the settings or make your own custom programs? Or do you want turn on and go simplicity?
4. How healthy/strong are you?
5. Do you want it to be water/weatherproof?
6. Do you want it to have wireless headphones and pinpointer capabilities?

The more times you've said yes, the more the price goes up.

Budget

As you've learned already, you don't have to spend a lot on a detector to get started, but do yourself a favor and don't buy any detector under $150. These machines are meant for children and while they will detect metal, that's all they do. Stick with the major manufacturers in the hobby, even the entry level machines from major manufacturers are good machines. There are many manufacturers out there; however, I can only recommend those I am familiar with—Minelab, Garrett, Tesoro, Fisher, and White's. This is not to denigrate other manufacturers; I just have not personally used them and therefore cannot recommend them.

If you have the funds or you're sure you'll like the hobby, then go ahead and start right off with a mid-level machine. This class of machine will give you all of the functionality of a top-of-the-line machine but with less customization of the performance and programming.

If a thousand dollars or more doesn't mean that much to you, or you have to have the best, then go ahead and get a high-end machine. Just keep in mind that the high-end machine will have a much steeper learning curve and won't guarantee you make any better finds. But you will have a top-of-the-line machine!

Types of detecting

If you plan on detecting parks and private lawns, any type of machines will work well.

If you want to work salt beaches, you'll need a multi-frequency machine at least, if not a pulse induction machine. If you plan on getting into the salt water, then you'll obviously need a waterproof machine and may want to consider a pulse induction machine.

If you want to metal detect farm fields or woods, you'll want a machine with a variety of larger coils available, all major manufacturers have these.

Weight

This is about the machine's weight, not yours.

The lightest machines come in around two and a half pounds. They feel incredibly light but, trust me, after a few hours of swinging them back and forth they don't feel so light anymore. Light machines are generally entry level machines and are not very sturdy and lack bells and whistles.

More sophisticated machines can be sturdier and can eclipse five pounds. This may not sound like a lot of weight, but try picking up a five-pound weight and swinging it back and forth for the next four hours. It gets heavy quickly. That extra weight comes with a sturdier body that can handle the inevitable bumps into rocks and trees and packs more bells and whistles with it, though, so it may be worth it for you.

Wireless accessories

It is becoming increasingly common for detectors to come with headphones and even pinpointers that are wirelessly connected to your headphones. They are worth every penny in my opinion, but they do add cost.

In the end, your budget, health, strength, and what you want to do with your machine mostly lead to the right detector for you. Your desires will narrow the field down to just a few models and all you have to do is pick one of those. Machines today are so much better than those of the past that you really can't go wrong no matter which one you choose.

What your detector tells you

Your detector provides a lot of information to you to help you determine what your target may be. *May be*. It is up to you to determine whether or not to retrieve the target.

Audio tone

When a target is located, your machine will give you a tone. The more sophisticated the machine, the more tones it'll give. An entry level machine may have only two tones and a top-of-the-line machine may have five or more. These tones are tied to what type of metal is being detected. Learning the tones of your machine will give you an indication of the type of metal below your coil.

Target ID number

Your machine will display a number when a target is located. Typically, this number ranges between 0 and 99 but some manufacturers use other numbers. These numbers correspond to various metals and give you more information on what may be below your coil. Iron is represented by low numbers followed by gold, nickel, aluminum, lead, copper and brass, and, lastly, silver.

Target indicator

Many machines will indicate what the programming suspects the target is, often with an icon. It may indicate that a coin, pull tab, or ring is under your coil. This is a best guess based on the size and metallic makeup of the target. This is by no means fully reliable.

Depth indicator
Most machines will give you a depth indicator. It can be as simple as shallow, medium, and deep or it could indicate a number of inches

below the surface the target may be. This can be very useful information in a public park, for instance, as you may choose not to dig very shallow targets that are likely to be recent drops, generally pennies and bottle caps.

As you gain experience with your machine, you will begin to decipher what it is telling you. The combination of audio tone, target ID number, and the target indicator will give you a lot of information to consider as to whether or not you want to recover the target. Some of the more interesting or unusual finds will come when these three pieces of information come in unusual combinations, so don't rely too much on this information, consider it a guide. The most important piece of information is that your machine has located a metal object. The more of those you choose to recover, the better your finds will be.

Search coils

When you bought your detector, it likely came with a single stock coil. You may have purchased a package that came with multiple coils and each has their advantages and disadvantages.

Small coils

Often called a sniper coil, small coils are generally six inches or less in diameter. The advantage they offer is a smaller search field, which is ideal for trashy areas such as public parks and some yards. These smaller search areas allow you to find good targets in between the junk. In a trashy park, you'll be better able to find the good items masked by bottle caps, pull tabs, and random junk items. What you give up with a small coil is depth.

Large coils

Large coils are anything from ten or eleven inches in diameter and bigger. Some coils are as large as seventeen inches or more in diameter. The advantage these coils have is a larger field that penetrates deeper—the main reason for such coils—and they cover more area. These coils are generally used on farm fields or in wooded areas for greater depth and coverage. The disadvantages are that they are heavy and lack the target separation of smaller coils. In a farm field or wooded area, target separation is rarely an issue since a diligent hunter usually goes after almost any target.

Stock coils

The coil your detector came with was likely between eight and ten inches in diameter. This size is a compromise between a small and large coil giving some of the advantages of each. Stock coils are generally speaking utility coils and they're pretty good in most situations. This is not to say they're not good, I use my stock coil at least 75% of the time, and you just need to understand that they lack the separation of a smaller coil and the depth of a bigger one.

There will be times when you want a sniper or large coil instead of the stock; unless or until you're very serious about the hobby your stock coil will suit you fine.

Know your machine

You need to know your machine. I mean really know your machine. The first thing to do is read your manual multiple times until you understand all of the functions. It wouldn't be a bad idea to spend a little time on YouTube searching for tutorials on your specific machine.

People often want a quick fix, the easy way out, and believe the "easiest way" is to buy a new/better machine. At least that's what the manufacturers want you to think. Trust me, the best set of brushes won't make you the next Picasso and the best set of golf clubs won't make you the next Rory Mc Elroy, but enough practice and knowledge of your machine just might.

When I first got serious about the hobby, everyone was rushing out to buy the Fisher F75; it's still a darn good machine. Then it was the Minelab CTX 3030, then the Garrett AT, then the XP Deus, and as of this writing it's the Minelab Equinox 800. And in a year or two it'll be another machine. I won't be buying any of them because my detector and I are a well-oiled machine.

The best thing you can do to improve the performance of your machine is to improve the performance of the operator—YOU. You need to read your manual inside and out until you know it cold. You need to spend time swinging your machine.

Building a test garden in your yard to practice on is a great idea.

A test garden is a place in your yard you've cleaned out all of the metal signals from. Then you can place various items at various depths so that you can practice going over them with your detector to know how your machine responds to them. Consider marking them with a golf tee so you know what is where; just push that tee right down to flush in the ground. Bury a coin lying flat, another standing on its edge, put a silver coin next to a bottle cap, nail, pull tab or other piece of junk metal to see if your machine can separate the good from the bad. Using your test garden regularly can hone your skills and improve your finds out in the field.

Read forums about your model and learn from others. Your machine is throwing a lot of info at you; audio tone, VDI, target depth, and target ID. Your machine cannot identify everything for you and you need to learn to interpret what it's telling you.

My Minelab Safari was easy to learn, but it took two years before I began to feel that I really understood what it was telling me. After years of using this machine now, there is still an occasional instance where I run into a combination of audio, VDI, and target ID that I've rarely or never seen. I still keep learning more about it all the time. You will need to do the same.

There are no shortcuts. The best way to get the most out of your machine is to know your machine well and that takes time.

When the next great machine comes out, keep in mind that every time you buy a new machine with the latest bells and whistles it's like learning a new language, you'll face a learning curve. I'm not against new technology—I'd like an Equinox 800 myself—but understand that the new tech will cost you hundreds if not over a thousand dollars and there is no guarantee that it will perform any better than your current detector. You'll need many hours to learn what this machine is telling you, when you could be out making finds with your current detector. It's the magician not the wand that makes the magic happen, remember that. Now go spend more time swinging whatever machine you have until you better understand what it is telling you. It will pay off in better and more finds.

Target recovery

Before you do anything, you need to know how to get an object out of the ground without killing grass. Notice I did not use the word "dig," don't use that word, especially when asking for permission on private property.

Every profession, occupation, and hobby has its own language and metal detecting is no different. "Dig" is the one word that you want to avoid when talking about the hobby with people who don't metal detect, doubly so if asking for permission.

We do not dig items, we retrieve them, we recover them, sometimes we even rescue them, but we do not dig them. You will not see that dirty word anywhere else in this book for a very good reason.

"Why is this?" you ask. Because when using that dirty word, it can immediately put into a landowner's mind the idea of a large shovel tearing into their lawn or backyard and many people will not like that idea at all.

Never use the dirty word when asking for permission to detect a property. If you have to mention at all how things get unearthed use the word "recover" or "retrieve" in reference to the target or artifact. It puts a much nicer spin on things and is much less likely to get you a "no" than the dirty word ever will.

So how do you retrieve an object then? It depends on where you are.

Farms, Fields, and Forests

If you're in a wooded area, a farm, or large fields (not parks) then a shovel is not only perfectly acceptable but preferable. You don't have to worry about damaging a lawn or being overly cautious, and the larger tool just makes it easier to get to your target. This is especially true if the target is deep. Of course, always replace your plug, remove your trash, and leave the land as you found it.

Public Places and Private Lawns

This is where you need to be on your game because if you do this wrong, you will damage the grass.

The first rule is do not recover targets from someone's lawn or a park during a drought; you will "kill" the grass. Don't do it during the heat of summer, either, as the grass is stressed and having its roots cut into will "kill" the grass as well.

"Kill" is in quotes because the grass will recover eventually, the following spring or fall, but you will leave behind a brown spot of dead grass. This will not make the landowner happy and in public places it's a good way to get the hobby banned in your town or city.

Only hunt lawns or parks in the spring, fall, and winter. The summer is best avoided.

So how do you retrieve a target?

The first thing to do is pinpoint the target as precisely as possible. Next, make a six to eight-inch "U" or "C"-shaped cut around the target leaving the target in the center. Make sure that the blade of your digging tool goes straight down; do not cut a cone-shaped plug. This is because a lawn mower can easily pull a cone-shaped plug out of the ground sending dirt everywhere and leaving a hole and an unhappy owner or park ranger behind.

Once you have your cut made, use your digging tool to pop the plug out of the ground leaving the open end of the "U" or "C" still attached to the ground like a hatch. This preserves some of the roots and helps the grass recover from being cut into.

If you've done a good job, the target will likely be in the plug and you can use your pinpointer to locate it within the plug and then push the plug back into the ground, step on it to push it down and go on your way.

The target may be deeper than your plug or just outside of the hole in the side wall. In this case, you will need to remove soil and it is important to manage this soil well. Many people use a "ground cloth" to put on the ground next to the hole to put excavated soil on so it can be easily poured back into the hole once the target is found. I prefer to use a piece of cardboard about the size of a piece of paper and fold it in half making it much easier to pour the soil back into the hole.

If done correctly, there will be no evidence of you having opened the ground. Practice this on your own lawn until you get good at it. Don't go to a public park or detect someone's yard unless you can recover a target without leaving evidence of your presence.

There are two oddities to remember about target recovery in a lawn. First, grass is very hardy and it will eventually grow back and turn green even if you've "killed" it. But you don't want to do this to someone else's yard or a park. Secondly, the bigger the plug you cut, the less harm you do to the grass. This is because when you cut a bigger plug, a smaller percentage of the grass in the plug is impacted by the cut. The problem with this is that cutting big plugs looks bad to the public who doesn't know better. So, when hunting in public and someone is around, try to cut a six-inch plug. But if no one is around, cut an eight or ten-inch plug as it's easier on the grass and makes target recovery easier as well.

Beaches

There are two approaches here, a beach sifter or a shovel. I prefer a shovel in most instances.

In the dry sand, many people go with a beach sifter. The dry sand easily flows through the sifter and leaves the target behind, assuming the target isn't too deep. If you'll only work the dry sand, then a sifter is a good idea.

In wet sand, a sifter is a lot harder to use as the wet sand doesn't flow through it so easily, the sand is heavy, and it's tougher to retrieve a target in. Many people do this, but I always use a shovel in the wet sand.

In the water is a different animal. If you don't have a waterproof machine, you can still work up to knee-deep water. Most people will use a long-handled beach scoop in this situation. On occasion, I will hunt the shallows, and I use a shovel since I don't feel the need to put money into a good sifter when I rarely go into the water.

If you do have a waterproof machine, and you do go out into the water, then a sifter is the only way to go. It would be virtually impossible to recover a target from waist or chest-deep water without using one. They're not cheap but are definitely necessary if you're going to be a water hunter.

A quick note about beaches. Don't be afraid to pick up and remove trash from the beach. Don't skip over it; that trash could easily be masking nearby targets that you would want to recover. Plus, it's just the right thing to do.

On one hunt, I saw a piece of iron lying on the surface that was about four inches square. I picked it up, put it in my pouch and ran my coil over where it had just been. To my surprise, a nice, clear signal rang out and just below the surface was a Barber quarter. Picking up trash is not only good for the planet but could be good for you as well.

Another thing to consider is that you will find a lot of lead sinkers. I keep them and throw them in a bucket in my garage until it's full. Lead is really bad for the environment, and I feel good about removing it. Lead isn't terribly valuable, but you can take it to a scrap yard and get a few bucks for helping to clean up the environment. Everyone wins.

Where to hunt

Now that you have your equipment and have learned what your machine is telling you, it's time to find a place to detect.

There are people who wonder where to go metal detecting or even those who will state there is "no place good around here to hunt." For the life of me, I can't understand this mentality as I have so many places on my list to hunt that I won't live long enough to hunt them all.

The first thing to do is download Google Earth to your computer and/or phone. Every time you find a good spot to check out, drop a pin on the location and add notes to it as to why you think it's a good location. When the next opportunity to get out there comes, you'll have plenty of places to choose from.

So where should you hunt? Start with your own yard and learn how to properly recover a target. Once you can recover a target without killing your yard, ask your family, friends, and neighbors to hunt their yards, especially if they have an older home. In this case, by older I mean anything built before 1960 as there is a chance to find silver coins there. Even if they don't have an older home, the land it's built on is old. Lots of farms get bought and turned into neighborhoods, and old coins and relics can be found in the yards of modern homes, so hit them. Just before printing this book, I was metal detecting a private school built in the 1930s and recovered a King George II farthing. It was too far gone to get a date off of, but these coins were minted between 1727 and 1760. What was a mid-eighteenth century coin doing in a twentieth century lawn? My guess is that the land was a farm in the past; you just never know what might show up under your coil.

Here is a list of places to hunt to get you thinking in the right direction.

Public Parks
Ball Fields
Beaches
Swimming Holes
Picnic Grounds
Roadside Rest Areas
Campgrounds
Fair Grounds
Curb Strips (the strip of grass between a sidewalk and the street)
Sidewalk Tear Outs (old sidewalks being removed)
Road Construction Sites (after the workers leave)
Old Schools
Old Churches
Old Walking Paths
Wooded Areas
Along Stone Walls
Ghost Towns
Cellar Holes
Cart Paths
Paper Roads
Farm Fields
Old Homes
Abandoned Property

Anywhere you can think of that people have been in the past, especially if they were there in big numbers, is a good place to detect. Once you start thinking about it, new sites will literally jump out at you and you'll always have places to go. And remember to mark them on Google Earth.

A last note before we end this topic. *Do not detect in cemeteries.*

Just don't do it. It's disrespectful, inconsiderate, and the optics of it are horrible. Remember, you are the face of the hobby and how you behave reflects on us all.

If the above doesn't deter you, remember cemeteries are mostly private property and, at the very least, you could be prosecuted for trespassing, not to mention desecrating a grave.

Old-school research

Once you have your equipment, have built your test garden, and know what kinds of places to look for, it's time to find some locations.

Let's start with old-school research.

Not everything is on the internet, not by a long shot, and that's a good thing for you. The easier a location is to find, the more likely it is that someone else has already beaten you to it. Someone beating you to a location doesn't mean it's hunted out, but it may mean that many of the targets are gone, at least the easy ones are.

So how do you find locations to hunt that don't show up easily on the internet? Your first step is to start close to home.

If you're fortunate enough to still have your parents, grandparents, or even great-grandparents, talk to them. If you're looking for silver coins like I usually am, then you need to talk to people who have personal memories of the days before 1965 when US dimes, quarters, half dollars and dollar coins were silver.

I was born in 1969 and obviously don't remember the silver era, but my parents graduated from high school in 1964 and 1965, so they do. I've asked them where they hung out after school, or on Friday nights, where they played, swam, and fished as kids. And when my grandparents were alive, I asked them the same things. I only wish I'd been into the hobby when the only great-grandparent I knew was still around as she did not pass until I was twenty-two. I'll never know that part of her history and what great leads could have come from it.

There is a lot you can ask people that may generate leads. What were the popular swimming holes in town? Where did people go fishing? Were the athletic fields in town in the same location or have they moved? Did a carnival come to town every summer and, if so, where? Where was the

"lovers' lane" that young people used to frequent? Did the town have fairs and/or town picnics? What about church picnics? Are there woods that you played in as a kid that haven't been developed? Did their parents or grandparents tell any stories about fairs, picnics, carnivals and the like from when they were kids? The older the better and the more people that were at an event the better. Are there any town legends about buried treasure, lost fortunes, banks robbed? Look into those.

If you don't have parents, or they don't generate any leads, there are plenty of older people you can talk to. Engage them in public, they'll love it. Granted, they might not get to the info you want right away, but just let them talk and tell you of the days past, you'll be surprised what leads may come up. And if you don't run into any octogenarians, stop by the local retirement home and see who is up for talking about the past. You never know what leads may happen and even if they don't produce any leads, you'll be making someone's day.

Another great resource to check out is your local library. Most have a local history section where you may be able to access documents not available anywhere else. These can be a valuable resource for leads. Read them with an inquisitive mind and see what may lead you to a great location. Check out any town maps they may have. Look at the local newspaper from way back when. This is a great place to find ads about the upcoming 4th of July picnic or a carnival, bonfire, or other big public event. One of the favorite kids' activities in the past was to put a huge pile of hay in a field and throw a bunch of coins in it and let the little ones find them. It kept them busy for a long time, and I guarantee you they didn't find them all. It's very likely that some of those coins are still there just waiting to be found.

Your current, local newspaper may run a weekly article on "twenty-five years ago" as well as fifty and even a hundred. Obviously for silver coins you'd need more than fifty years ago, but you get the point.

Arcadia Publishing produces an enormous number of local history books written by locals. Your town may have one and the local library probably has a copy. They're mostly pictorial histories, so look through them seeking places to metal detect. You may find images of company picnics, town fairs, festivals, feasts, church retreats, and summer concerts; anyplace people gathered in the past will likely hold treasures to be found.

If your town has a local historical society it's worth checking out. Consider becoming a member or at least talk to the members. It's entirely possible they have an official town historian; this is definitely someone you want to talk to.

These are just some of the ways to find great places to hunt via "old-school" methods. The more research you do, the easier it will become to find new places to hunt.

Internet research

The good news about the internet is that there is a massive amount of information out there that can help you locate great places to metal detect. What's not so great is that this information is available to anyone with internet access. So it's not exactly obscure information you're working with here. This is why I love old-school research so much. But let's consider the internet.

Your town or city real estate database can be very helpful in determining ownership of land and the age of buildings as well. Just keep in mind that these are not always entirely up to date. Sometimes you may notice that a lot of houses in an older neighborhood were built in "1900." This often means they have no exact records but it was probably built somewhere in that general time frame, give or take fifteen or twenty years.

These websites are all national and have all been very helpful for me. You can likely find others specific to your area that will have other info as well. Try Googling your town and "old map" or "history" for starters.

www.historicmapworks.com : This is a great site that allows you to layer historic maps over modern satellite imagery. It's great for finding cellar holes in the woods or where buildings and roads used to be.

www.historicaerials.com : This site has aerial photos from all over the country. There are more in the east and especially in urban areas, but there are photos going back to the 1930s and it's great for seeing how areas changed over time. One of my favorite ways to use this is looking for baseball fields that are no longer present. Every town had multiple baseball fields in the past when the game truly was

America's pastime and people lost lots of coins and other items in these fields.

www.acrevalue.com It's free to join the basic level and even that gives you information on farms including the name of the owner, which can be very helpful in gaining permission. If you pay to join, there is further information available such as what the land has been used for and, I believe, how long.

www.archives.gov/research The national archive has all kinds of information such as maps and photos that can be helpful for leads. In the photos section you can just enter the name of your town and see what comes up.

www.landmarkhunter.com Helps you find prominent landmarks, which can be helpful in the field.

www.usgs.gov/products/maps/topo-maps Topographical maps of the whole country.

www.oldmapsonline.com Just like it says, punch in a city or address and see what they have.

www.google.com/maps Has up-to-date satellites of the world today. This is good for basic reconnaissance on a location and allows you to drop electronic pins and notes on the map that you can access from the field on your phone. You'll need to tie a Google email address to your phone to do this though.

www.bing.com/maps Also has modern satellite images, but Bing allows you to rotate the image, which sometimes gives away features of the land you wouldn't see on Google Earth. It also seems to have more winter images that allow you to see forests without a canopy and find stone walls more easily.

www.zillow.com :You can learn a lot about a home here. Most importantly, you can learn the age of the house but also the size of the lot as well.

www.onxmaps.com This is my favorite website/app and it wasn't even designed for metal detecting. It was designed for hunting. What it does so well for our hobby is show property boundary lines and who owns the land in most jurisdictions. The best part is that once you've found a location, you can outline it on the app and see the boundaries on your phone so you are sure you're still on the property you have permission to be on. What I use it for most is having all of my locations identified on the map, so whenever I have the time to get out, I never have to think of where to go. I just look at the app and see what's near me of interest.

Leads are everywhere

If you're just starting out, or even a veteran detectorist, you may struggle with thinking of places to go. The easiest way to find places to detect is simply to be aware of your surroundings and keep an eye out for interesting places to detect as you go about your normal life.

An unusually good example of this happened to me in January of 2019. I was driving home with my family one day, coming from a direction we rarely travel, when we drove by a large lake I'd seen a number of times before. What caught my eye this time was that the lake was unusually low exposing at least twenty feet of shoreline. I made a mental note to do some research later on.

A few days later, I started looking into the lake and discovered that it is man-made and controlled. It is, in fact, lowered in the winter. Further research found a small neighborhood on the shore of the lake that contained about forty small beach houses that were almost all built in the 1930s. Figuring this place had potential for modern silver coins and some jewelry I planned a hunt with a hunting partner of mine.

Unfortunately, when we arrived at the lake a few days later, the level of the lake had changed significantly. We had two days of good rain in the previous week and I couldn't believe how much the lake had come up. More than half of the previously exposed lake bottom was again under water. But we were there so we decided to give it a go.

The first area we hit was loaded with old bricks, mid-century glass, and some pottery so it held potential. But after a while of digging nothing but junk, we decided to move on to the section of the lake right in front of the old beach houses.

Targets were few and far between due to the amount of sand they had brought in over the years to make a sandy beach. We worked away from the swimming area digging most pennies, but eventually I got a good signal. It initially hit 39 on my target ID, which typically indicates a quarter before locking in at 36. A 36 signal is typically a wheat penny or copper Lincoln but can on occasion be a silver dime as well. I figured it was a wheat penny and stuck my shovel into the lake bottom. Initially, I couldn't find the coin in the hole or the dirt pile excavated from the hole. That was awfully odd. Then I saw a quarter-sized grey disk standing on edge between two rocks. It had popped out of the hole as I removed my shovel. Based on the age of the houses, I figured that might be a Standing Liberty quarter. The coin was rather encrusted so I walked over to the water to rinse it off.

To my surprise, when I lifted the coin out of the lake, I could see Seated Liberty clear as day under the black muck. This was only my second Seated Liberty quarter and while happy to have it, for some reason I wasn't overly excited. Walking over to my partner, I handed it to him and, needless to say, he was surprised. He noticed something that I had missed, the coin was holed, which further reduced my excitement. Looking at it myself, I noticed that it was a relatively common date of 1875, so I put it in my pants pocket and continued on. My partner asked if there was a mint mark on it, but I could not make it out due to the muck and, honestly, my "mature" eyes.

After about two hours of hunting the lake and only getting clad— and the one good find—we were wishing it was warmer and we had waterproof machines so we could get out there in chest-deep water and find some silver coins and jewelry, but it wasn't meant to be.

Arriving home, I showed my son my finds of the day, and the family went on with our normal evening. Later that evening, I remembered my partner commenting about a mint mark on the quarter so I got out my five power loop and took a look. To my surprise, a CC Mint mark was there sharp and crisp as could be. "Honey, it's a Carson City," I yelled to my wife who had no understanding of what that meant. Quickly looking it up, I saw that the 1875 CC quarter had a mintage of only 144,000. I was shocked; suddenly the "common date" Seated quarter took on a whole new meaning, I was over the moon! It took a good ten minutes for me to quell the excitement and begin to function again. Only my second Seated quarter ever and it was a Carson City! I started texting all of my metal detecting buddies and the congratulations started pouring in.

After getting the kids to bed and basking in the excitement of my find, I took out the loop to take a closer look and admire the find I'd made. That's when things got crazy.

Looking at the CC Mint mark, it occurred to me that it did not say "Quarter Dollar" below the mark but rather ... "Twenty ... Cents." I called my wife over to look at it because I couldn't believe what I was seeing.

"Does this say twenty cents?" I asked. I knew it did, but I just couldn't believe it.

Taking a look she said, "Yes it does."

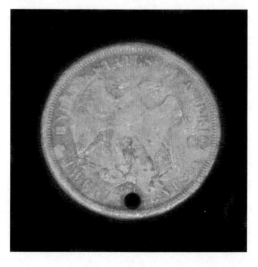

I went numb. All I could do was put my hands on my forehead and say, "Oh my God, oh my God, a Carson City twenty cent piece, oh my God." I couldn't say anything else and mostly just sat there in stunned silence for a good ten minutes. I was beyond words. The 1875 Carson City twenty cent piece has a mintage of 133,290.

Like most in this hobby, I've dreamed of someday finding a gold coin, and it could happen. But this coin wasn't even on my bucket list it's so rare, yet there it was sitting on my dining room table. And this coin is now in my collection because I simply made a mental note of something I saw while driving home with my family.

On another occasion, my wife and I were traveling down a road we had traveled many times, but this time it was late fall and the leaves were down making it easier to see into the woods. Driving down the road, out of the corner of my eye, I saw something stone and man-made flash by in the woods. I made a mental note of where we were on the road so I could slow down on the way back and get a better look.

Traveling back home, I paid close attention to where we were on that road and slowed down to get a better look. Sure enough, in the woods were two stone fireplaces that could not be seen when the leaves were on the trees. I knew the road was old and, when I got home, I decided to look at some old aerial photographs of the area. On a 1939 aerial, I could see that the area in question was not wooded then and the fireplaces were present. The history of the location seemed to be a roadside rest area in the days before the interstate system.

A few days later, I went back with detector in hand to check the area out. There were not a lot of signals making me think the area had been hunted before. Being so close to the road this was highly likely. But fairly quickly I started to hit a few wheat pennies and I knew my predecessors didn't get it all.

Near one of the stone fireplaces, I dug a Mercury dime though there wasn't much else around. I continued to work around the area not finding much other than a half dozen or so wheat pennies and I started to follow a small creek away from the roadside area. Near the base of a small tree, I got a really good signal that I was very confident was silver. Digging down, I quickly hit roots and knew this one would be a tough recovery. If the signal had been less clear and solid, indicating silver, I might have decided it didn't warrant the work, but I decided to keep going. After digging through several inches of roots and finding the target literally between two roots, a 1953 Roosevelt dime came to the surface. The site didn't produce any more silver, just a few clad coins and a couple more wheat pennies, but it was well worth the time.

This all circles back to being aware of where you are and what is around you. Wherever I go, a portion of my attention is always scanning the area looking for places to detect. Stone walls grab my attention, as do farms, old houses and any body of water. People always gravitate to water and lose things along the shore or riverbank. If you simply keep your eyes open with a mind towards metal detecting as you go through your normal life's activities, you'll find plenty of places to detect.

Gaining permission for private property

Public parks have been hunted by everyone since the 1960s, so if you want to consistently find older coins, relics, and jewelry, you need to get on private land.

For a number of reasons people are afraid of or don't know how to ask for permission on private property. I have to admit that even at this stage of my involvement in the hobby, it can sometimes be uncomfortable. You have to get over this. If one landowner says no, that's no big deal, there are countless other landowners to ask, so go ask them.

A good approach to this is to target a promising neighborhood and keep asking until you get a yes. One way to mitigate the uncomfortable feeling of knocking on a stranger's door is to do it with a hunting partner or two. I don't mean that two or three of you knock on someone's door as that may be counterproductive, or worse; rather, take turns knocking on doors until one of you gets a yes.

One day, my buddies, Ron and Pete, and I went to a neighborhood I had targeted because of the large number of old homes in it. Thankfully they were with me because every door I knocked on that day I got one of three responses. The most common was no response as nobody answered the door, followed by, "My friend/brother, cousin/whomever has one of those and he wants to do it," and lastly a straight "No." Thankfully both Ron and Pete got a "yes" for us that day and we had plenty of land to detect.

Private land really is the last frontier for metal detecting unless you're going to learn to scuba dive and buy underwater equipment. I'm a big fan of unfettered access to oxygen so I'll stick to private permissions on land.

How do you get permission to hunt private land?

First, you have to do your research and find a location that is worth your time. The easiest "research" is to go to the oldest part of your town and start knocking on doors. Don't be intimidated, just figure out what you're comfortable with saying and doing and go do it. Door knocking isn't the easiest thing for some people to do; here are a few suggestions to keep in mind.

Don't knock on someone's door too early in the morning or late in the day. Don't show up on someone's doorstep covered in dirt and sweat because you've been metal detecting in the heat for hours, and don't carry your equipment to the door, leave it in the car. You can and should be dressed to start right then if you get the OK, just don't be a mess.

Once you've chosen a house, knock on the door or ring the bell and step back a few feet so that you're not seen as a threat. And if you're wearing a hat, take it off, especially in the South and Midwest where manners still matter.

If someone answers the door, don't be nervous, you're not asking for their daughter's hand in marriage, just to detect their land.

Relax and be yourself, but keep in mind they have no idea who you are, why you're there, or what you want. Get to the point of why you're there and ask for permission. You need to practice enough to be smooth with your sales pitch. Depending on the situation I've got a few basic approaches.

1. "Hi, sorry to bother you, my name is Brian and I'm a metal detecting hobbyist and I look for older homes like yours to metal detect. Would you mind if I detected your property?"

That's it, done. Wait for their response.

2. "Hi, sorry to bother you. First off, I'm not selling anything or running for office. (Smile) My name is Brian and I'm a history buff, my hobby is metal detecting and I use a handheld machine to locate metal objects in the ground. Would you mind if I detected your property?

   Wait for their response.

3. "Hi, sorry to bother you, my name is Brian and I'm a history buff and huge fan of old houses like yours. I look for older houses for my hobby of metal detecting. They're great for finding old buckles, buttons, tools, all kinds of random metal items, and the occasional coin. Would you mind if I used my metal detector in your yard?"

4. "Hi, my name is Brian and I was metal detecting your neighbor Steve's yard and he thought you might let me check out your yard as well if that's OK?" This is, of course, assuming you actually were at Steve's house earlier.

Sometimes, after your spiel, a yes comes, sometimes a no, other times you're met with confusion or questions. If it's confusion or a question, I further explain that "I'm a history buff and I enjoy finding everyday items from the past like buttons, buckles, coins, and all types of man-made objects. I'll also likely remove a lot of junk metal from your yard as well if that's OK with you."

Who wouldn't want free junk removal?

You might want to spend a few dollars and have some business cards made up. Put your name, phone number, and email address on it along with a phrase like "Metal Detecting Specialist" or "Relic Recovery" or any other phrase you come up with to describe the hobby. Put the code of ethics on the back as well so they know you won't damage their property. This gives you an air of professionalism as well as your contact info, which tends to put people at ease.

If you're really interested in a property, and aren't afraid to use a little emotional blackmail, bring your child along and explain how this is a hobby and a love of history that the two of you share. Tug on their heartstrings all you can; my buddy and his teenage son are into the hobby and he has phenomenal success with this approach.

If a property is owned by a corporation or organization you might have a bit of a challenge getting to the person who can grant permission, and you may have no choice but to do it by phone. Phone calls and emails are much less successful than face-to-face meetings in my opinion, but I have had success this way. Just get to the point as no one wants to read a long email or hear a long sales pitch.

Private property really is the final frontier of the hobby. It's the only place where you have a reasonable chance of being the first person ever to swing a detector over the soil. So get over your fear and just go do it. You'll get your share of no's but you'll be surprised how many times you'll hear, "Sure."

Don't call city hall

You've done your research and found a great location on public land. Maybe it's an old fairground, or where the circus used to perform, or where socials were held in the past or any other public event. These are all good spots. But they can present a problem.

Sometimes, well-meaning people can do things that hurt themselves or, in this case, the hobby of metal detecting. These well-meaning people might call town or city hall and attempt to speak to the mayor or head of parks and recreation and ask the very reasonable question, "Is metal detecting allowed on town-owned land?"

Do not do this.

"Why?" you ask.

Put yourself in the position of the deputy assistant to the mayor's lackey who ends up fielding your call. I can all but guarantee you two things. First, that person doesn't know if there is an ordinance or not. And, second, that person will think to themselves, *What could go wrong if I say yes?* Then they envision some fool with a huge shovel digging enormous holes in town parks or athletic fields and them having to answer to the head of Park & Rec. or the mayor as to why they said yes. What would you do? You'd probably say no as well.

This is why you don't call city hall to ask permission to metal detect public land. So what do you do?

These days, every town of any size has a website. Contained within their website is a section on Parks & Rec. or town regulations. Read those and look for any reference to metal detecting restrictions, there likely aren't any. Or you can be lazy (efficient in my book) and open the rules and regs and hit the control button while holding down the "f" button and open a search box. Then search for the words detector, detecting, and metal.

If there is anything there about the hobby, it'll show up. But it's very unlikely that your town has any ordinances. You'll want to know this in advance before metal detecting public land, especially if it's easily viewable by the public such as a park or ballfield.

If you want to be extra prepared, print out the rules and regulations for the town and have them in your car to show to any law enforcement, town workers, or nosey people who may question you. It's good to know you're OK when that person with nothing better to do than tell you that you can't metal detect in a public park shows up.

Most importantly, keep in mind that you are not doing anything illegal, so you don't need to ask permission to do it. Think of it this way, have you ever asked permission to walk across or into a public park before? How about throwing a ball with you child? Why would you? It's public!

Site reading

Now you're ready to do some metal detecting. You've chosen your equipment, done your research, found a promising location and have secured permission to hunt it if it's private land or confirmed there are no ordinances if it's public land.

So now what?

You're on location, where do you start to search? Do you just wander randomly or are there spots more likely to produce good finds than others? It depends on the location, how much research you've done, and how much time you have.

Hopefully you've looked at old maps to get an idea of what the land may have been like in the past. If you're lucky there are older photos on www.historicaerials.com and you have identified areas that are of interest to you. Let's take a look at different types of locations.

Private homes

I've always had the most success in the front yard of homes. Start with the area leading from the driveway to the front, back, and/or side doors. People are going into their pockets coming from and going to the car and things get dropped. I also like to look at the street and imagine where I would park if I were a guest and work from there to the front door. Around mailboxes is a great spot as well. In the distant past, when postage was a penny, people would leave a letter in the box and an Indian Head penny to cover the postage. Surely many of those hit the ground.

In the backyard, I always start with two places. First is fanning out from the back door as, again, people come and go from there in all directions with their hands going into and coming out of their pockets. Second is the clothesline as coins often made it through the wash in pockets before being inverted on the line and falling out.

Granted, most people don't use clotheslines anymore, but look for the evidence of where one would have been in the past. Look for hooks or pulleys near windows. If none exist, look for an older tree close enough to a window for it to have been used as a clothesline, work these areas and you may be awarded with older coins or even a piece of jewelry.

If the home has a detached garage or shed then around them towards the house are good locations as well. Older homes sometimes have or had stone fireplaces in the backyard, work around these. If the home is older, pre-1960, and has large trees, then work under and around those trees as in the days before air conditioning people would seek refuge from the sun and heat of the house by sitting under a tree. My first Walking Liberty half dollar came from under a nice shady tree just out the back door of an old farmhouse.

If it is a large yard, look for any evidence of previous outbuildings such as rusty old nails or a depression in the ground to work around. And keep an eye out for those shady trees, the bigger and older the better. And look for stumps of long-dead trees or, even better, depressions where a stump was pulled out long ago. These are great places to metal detect.

If a yard is small, or particularly productive, you'll want to work a grid pattern. Search it east to west allowing your sweeps to overlap. Then search it north to south, again overlapping your swings. Finally, you may want to search it from a southeast or northwest approach as well to make sure you've covered every bit of ground. This is especially useful in small yards.

Wooded Areas

If you're working the woods and don't have a specific target area such as a known cellar hole or the remains of a chimney then there are still things to look for. The most obvious is stone walls as they didn't build themselves and indicate that someone was there for a long time. Walls typically get more refined once they get within a few hundred feet of where a home was, so pay attention to the wall itself as you work near it.

Keep an eye out for water. Streams always draw people to them and you should work alongside them. Ponds or other small bodies of water were used for animals, swimming, and fishing and should be checked out as well. In colonial times, a home site was commonly built within a short distance of a water supply be it a stream, river or pond. It was also common for a home to be built on a high point overlooking the surrounding area and/or water supply. Look for these high points near water, especially if they're relatively flat on top and a good place to build a home.

While in the woods, keep an eye out for nonnative trees, plants, and flowers. They didn't plant themselves there, a human did, and they planted them in their yard. While in the woods, and especially if near walls, keep an eye out for any trees that are significantly larger and older than the others in the area. This may be an indication of a tree that was in a cleared yard in the distant past but is now surrounded by younger trees—work around that tree.

When you're in the woods, don't discriminate out iron targets. Iron is your friend. Iron junk tells you there has been human activity in the area. When you hit iron, slow down and retrieve it all. Retrieve it because lots of good relics are iron and because that iron in the ground can mask targets made of other metals like silver and gold.

Public Parks

For some reason many detectorists fire up their machines and head out to the middle of a park upon their arrival. It's not that good things can't be found anywhere in a park because they can, but I suggest you take some time to think about how you will hunt the park.

If you've looked at old aerial photos you may see footpaths that no longer exist, go to where they were. You may also see playground equipment, ball fields, or other attractions that have moved or no longer exist, check those areas out too.

If you were waiting to meet a friend at the park, or catch a bus, trolley, or taxi, where would you wait? It's very likely that you'd meet near an entrance.

I always start at entrances and fan out into the park. Or you can start at parking areas and fan out towards attractions, ponds, hills, or other landmarks. Speaking of hills, look for good sledding hills and work the top and bottom of them. Targets can be in the middle as well, but most will be at the top or bottom where hats and gloves were put on and taken off and rings fell.

Find the athletic fields and look for good spots to sit and watch the game, detect this area. This could be a nearby shady tree or any elevation in ground affording a good view. People naturally seek these areas out and you should too.

No matter where you start, when you find a good target, slow down and work that area in a search pattern to see if it is a hotspot for items. Start by spiraling out from the target to see if there are more. If more good targets show up, consider working a grid on the area.

Farms

Work around the house as noted above in the section on houses. The big difference is that you're going to find a lot more iron around an old farmhouse than you would other houses.

As far as the farm itself is concerned there are a few things to look for. Find where the barn(s) and outbuildings were, if they're still standing even better. Work the areas between the main house and the buildings. There was a well near the house unless water is very close by. If the well is gone, covered, or filled, look for a small depression likely within fifty or sixty feet of the house. Look for a depression where the outhouse may have been. Outhouses moved from time to time as they got filled in, so there may be multiple outhouse locations. Search between them and the house.

Outhouses were always built downwind of the house for obvious reasons. So if you know which way the prevailing winds blow, you know which direction to search in. Also keep in mind how far you would want to walk from the house to use said outhouse, the answer is not very far.

The fields are a lot harder to pin down as far as good areas are concerned. One thing to look for are any lone trees in the fields. Farm workers would likely seek a little refuge from the sun under these for a drink, lunch, or a quick break. If there is a body of water of any kind on the property work from it back towards the house. No matter how you go about working the fields, if you find iron or a good target, slow down and work that area to see if there is more there.

Beaches

Beach hunting for recent drops

Let's start with modern stuff like jewelry, technology, and change. For these finds any beach currently in use will be just fine since you're looking for contemporary stuff. If your beach has dunes there are likely paths going through, around, or over the dunes. Work these paths as people are fumbling in their pockets going to or from their cars dropping change, rings and the occasional cell phone.

Work the "towel line". This is generally right above the high tide line as people like to get as close to the water as possible without getting wet so there is a clear line of demarcation where the towels start and end. Lots of items get left behind here.

Go out into the wet sand, especially at low tide in what would be knee-deep water at other points in the tide cycle. Why? Because people with small children will take them out in 12–18 inches of water for them to play in. These people have often just put sunscreen on their little ones making their fingers slippery and they lose rings. Even without sunscreen, when their hands hit the cold water, fingers shrink up and rings drop.

Obvious places of entrance and exit see the most traffic and need your attention. Also, near beach showers if present. Anywhere vendors may be are good and don't forget those lifeguard chairs. When the lifeguards aren't around, people like to climb up them for a better view and occasionally some amorous evening activity; things get dropped.

The best time to go is right after a big weekend or holiday. Don't wait for Monday morning; the early bird is there at the end of the day on Sunday. Make sure you're familiar with any regulations about

45

detecting public beaches before you go. In Rhode Island, for example, it's open season as long as the lifeguards are not on duty. So by 5 p.m. you're good to go and there is still plenty of light left to the day in the summer months.

Beach hunting for relics and silver coins

If you're looking for older stuff like relics and silver coins, then your approach needs to be a little different as they were not dropped earlier on the day of your arrival.

First, you need to be on a beach that has been in use for a long time or, conversely, one that hasn't been in use for a long time. The latter are often better. For various reasons a beach may have been popular in the past but isn't anymore. This could be industrial or other development leaving a beach no longer desirable or a natural disaster or fire of the past may have done in an old hotel or resort. This is a place you would be interested in for old coins, relics, and jewelry. Don't forget that in the past people didn't travel like we do now. So if a neighborhood is on the coast, they likely went to the little strip of sand at the end of the road rather than the big town or state beaches. Make sure to look for those little, sandy beaches.

For relics, you need to find a place that had lots of activity that wasn't sunbathing. It could be a shipyard, ferry landing, fishing port, railroad crossing, amusement park, clam shack, or anything else that brought people to the shore. You'll need to get familiar with the local history to find these places, do your research.

Second, you'll need to go at the right time. I usually go about two hours before low tide and work along the water line as the tide recedes then let the incoming tide push me back up the beach covering much of the same ground again. This doesn't mean you can't find relics halfway up the beach, at the high tide line or even above, because I have. But you want to take advantage of low tide to expose as much of the beach as possible. You can hunt the high tide line and above any time.

Third, you'll want to look for any obvious cuts or washouts, if they're there then work those. Rocks are your best friend, if you see a bunch of rocks on the beach head right for them. Rocks, coins and jewelry are all heavy and sink to the bottom; if rocks are on the surface then that is the bottom whether it's clay or bedrock. Lots of heavy items, including lead sinkers, will collect here.

You want to avoid deep sand. If you're walking on the wet sand and your feet are sinking in, you're on deep sand. In time you will learn to feel this with your feet. Take your shovel and periodically excavate to see how deep the sand around you is. If you go down a foot and haven't hit clay or ledge or bedrock, keep moving. The funny thing about sand depth is that you can have exposed clay or bedrock in one space and a few feet away the sand is a few feet deep. You never know how big an area of clay or bedrock is, so once you find it slow down and recover any signal that repeats.

Fourth, get to know your beach, this takes time. Beaches are dynamic environments and if you only go to a beach once you'll not really know anything about it. Wind, waves, and storms move sand onto and off of the beach. The direction the beach faces and the direction the wind or storm is coming from will impact whether sand moves in or out. Over time you will get to know a beach and will be able to tell simply by looking at it whether or not the sand has moved and in which direction.

If you go to a beach once, hunt it hard, and get skunked this really doesn't tell you much at all. Maybe you were in the wrong spot, maybe the sand was deep, maybe good items were masked by iron, or maybe you just didn't put your coil over a good target. The only way you will know this is by returning many times and getting to know the beach.

Finding silver coins and old relics comes down to choosing the right beach and getting to know it well. The time invested in finding the beach and getting to know it will be rewarded, eventually.

Don't ignore penny signals

Let's be honest, almost nobody wants to find modern pennies, especially zinc planchet pennies. Those Zincolns are so distinctive that many machines can pick them out, on mine they almost always ring in at a 34 and there is a strong temptation to ignore them. Admittedly, I ignore them at times depending on a lot of factors such as the location, how hard or rocky the ground is, and how much time is available. But this is to tell you why you shouldn't ignore obvious penny signals, at least not always.

There is a large public park not far from me that has produced good finds for decades and still does. Not long ago, I was there with my family and squeezed in a quick hunt of about thirty minutes, and in that time I got two wheat pennies and a 1962 Roosie. That's not exactly earth shattering, but for a half hour hunt it's pretty good.

A few years ago, I was hunting the park on a hot summer day. I'm not a fan of heat and really don't like the sun either, so I was confining my hunting to shaded areas under trees. One shaded hillside has a small rain washout area to it that I knew I'd hunted before. Since I was only hunting under trees that severely limited the amount of ground available to me, I was digging every signal. Right in the little washout I got a penny signal, recovered it and looked at a dirty copper disk. It looked like a penny and went into my pouch. It wasn't until I got home and ran the clad under some water that I noticed it wasn't a penny at all.

The coin turned out to be a Pro-Union store token from a place called Charlney's on Orange Street in Providence, RI. My first Civil War token came because I dug a signal that at times I would ignore, so the lesson was learned there.

On another occasion, at the same park, I was being good and digging all repeatable signals above iron when I dug a penny signal that brought up a strange looking, penny-sized coin. There was clearly a bust of Lady Liberty on the obverse, but it was a bust I'd never seen before. When I turned it over, I saw the words "Our Army" surrounded by a wreath. It was my second Civil War token and the second one I dug in the same park because of digging penny signals.

There are times when ignoring penny signals may make sense. depending on your goals, the location, and conditions, but don't let it become a habit. Remember, no detector is right all the time and you have to be willing to recover a lot of junk to find the good stuff.

"So when might it make sense to ignore penny signals?" you ask. It *might* make sense to ignore them if they are on the surface or are very shallow signals. You're pretty sure it's a penny and it's very shallow so it is highly likely that you're right, and it's likely a recently dropped, modern coin. It *might* make sense to ignore penny signals if you have limited time and your primary goal is silver coins. Other than those two specific scenarios, it's in your best interest to recover those penny signals, ignore them at your peril.

Persistence

Persistence pays off.

Don't be too quick to give up on a location just because you searched it for a certain amount of time and didn't find anything good.

On one occasion, I checked out a beach near my home and got nothing other than clad coins and trash. Over the next couple of months, I went back twice and got nothing but clad coins and trash and decided I'd given the beach enough time with nothing to show for it.

More than a year passed, and, one day, I found myself near the same beach with time on my hands and no leads nearby. Checking an online tide chart, I realized it was just before low tide and off to the beach I went.

Things were pretty slow for the first ninety minutes—more clad and trash—until, finally, I dug a quarter that was obviously silver as it was blackened and hard to identify. I took it to the water's edge to rinse it off and saw that it was a Standing Liberty quarter. This reinvigorated me and over the rest of the hunt, I dug five more silver coins.

A six silver hunt is a darn good day and I was back to the same beach the very next day. The second hunt there produced my highest silver count ever, nine Mercury dimes, a Barber dime, a Barber quarter and a silver Washington quarter!

For the better part of the next two years, that beach became my go-to location as it continued to produce silver coins before eventually drying up.

Another example comes from when I first started in the hobby; I had no success at a large public park that is popular with detectorists. The best I managed was a few wheat pennies now and then, but I kept going back because, at that point, I didn't know where else to go. As my skills improved, I began to get the occasional silver dime from the park.

What I now know is that the park still contains silver coins, but the "easy targets", such as half dollars, quarters, and shallow dimes, are likely all gone. Silver dimes are still there, but they're masked by fifty plus years of modern change, pull tabs, bottle caps, and miscellaneous junk. It takes a skilled and patient detectorist to find silver there, but it's still there.

Keep this in mind, just because you don't find anything good at a location on your first hunt, or second, or subsequent hunts doesn't mean there isn't anything good there. It just means you haven't found anything good there. There is a difference.

Thinking outside the park

Sometimes we have to get creative to find new places to metal detect.

There is a well-known, old, and large park not far from where I live. Over time, a lot of coins, jewelry, and other good items have been lost there, including the first Seated dime I ever found. It has been a detecting hotspot since detectors were first in use I'd guess.

It's one of the first places I went when starting out detecting and it produced a number of wheat pennies for me, which was great at the time. I did find a few pieces of silver jewelry and even a Civil War-era naval button. But eventually things changed in the park.

According to the scuttlebutt, a few years ago, some knucklehead went metal detecting in the park using a standard-sized spade shovel as his digging tool and left huge open holes in the park. The rumor is that he literally opened up holes with the spade, got his target, and left the enormous plugs lying next to the holes. As you might imagine, this made the park rangers less than happy and understandably they began telling people they could not detect in the park.

I got to experience this firsthand when a ranger told me that it was a "historic park" and we could use our detectors but could only recover items on the surface. That's kind of like saying you can dribble on the basketball court but can't shoot. As of this writing it's still unclear—to me at least—if detecting is actually banned by ordinance or law, but either way the rangers don't take kindly to people digging in the park and it's not worth an argument.

So what do you do when a prime location gets closed off to detecting? Do you go in anyway and risk getting detecting banned all over the city? Do you call city hall and complain knowing this might lead to further bans? Hint: don't do that. Do you go in at night and hunt in the dark? I don't recommend any of these, but here's what I did.

I figured that before World War II not a lot of people had cars, especially in a city with good public transportation. So it's likely that people came to the park on a trolley, bus, or by foot. So where are or were those trolley and bus stops? There would likely be good targets between the stops and the park. Unfortunately, I wasn't able to find any info on trolley or bus stops, but how else did people get to the park? The answer is a lot of them walked to the park. And while walking to the park you know they dropped things.

This got me thinking of where exactly people entered the park in the past. I've always liked hunting around the entrances to parks as that is where people would meet or catch their rides. I've never understood why people are in a rush to get to the middle of the park to turn on their machine as the concentration of people there is likely much less dense than at the entrances.

So how could I find out what entrances were most used or if there were ones no longer in existence? I turned to www.historicaerials.com. On a 1939 aerial, I discovered a clear walking path leading across a field towards one of the entrances. It was across the street from and outside of the park, so nothing to worry about from the rangers. The path also showed up on a 1955 aerial, but most importantly for those of us who love silver coins, it did not appear to be present on a 1963 aerial. It seemed that this path was in use during the silver era but disappeared thereafter, this was very good news. Also of note was a line of small trees in both photos that ran parallel to the street; though small, they likely provided shade for people waiting for a ride or simply seeking shelter from the sun. Looking at modern aerials, I noticed that only one of the trees still stood.

On my first trip there, I concentrated on working under and around that large tree and pulled the expected numbers of clad coins and junk targets before eventually getting rewarded for my effort and research. The first silver to come out of the ground was a 1945 Mercury dime and about fifteen feet away was a 1903 Barber dime. They were both in great shape so it's likely that those two pretty ladies had spent many a summer day relaxing under the shade of that big tree before I found them.

On subsequent hunts, I worked alongside the missing tree line with a buddy and we pulled a large number of wheat pennies, an Indian Head penny or two, a few more Mercury dimes, and a couple of Barber dimes.

Over following hunts we moved further along the path and away from the street and continued to find wheat pennies and a few Barber and Mercury dimes as well as a Walking Liberty half and a Depression-era food token. The finds were not overwhelming, but they were very satisfying as they came about from solid research and thinking outside the box, or the park in this case.

So when you hear that a place is "hunted out," don't believe them because it isn't. Learn to think outside the box, and you just may find yourself a piece of previously untouched land just waiting for the determined detectorists to find it.

Improving the quality of your finds

The best way to increase the quantity and quality of your finds is very simple, move slow, and excavate it all.

That's a lot easier said than done. Modern machines are excellent at discriminating out iron and good with foil, so it is very tempting to pass up targets, but you shouldn't. The reason why is because no machine is right all the time.

Iron, especially large pieces of iron, can mask other nearby targets. So you want to remove the junk iron. Some iron objects, such as tools, cannon balls, grapeshot, etc., are desirable and you want to recover them.

Your machine cannot tell the difference between pieces of aluminum foil and small gold rings, it also can't tell the difference between pull tabs and small gold rings. And most machines can't tell the difference between a pull tab and a nickel. You may not care much about nickels, but larger pieces of gold, such as a class ring, may ring up like a nickel. So if you want to consistently make good finds, you'll need to unearth a lot of junk.

The other thing you need to do to maximize your finds is to go low and slow. Low means keeping your coil as close to the ground as possible. On grass this means sweeping your coil so that it is in contact with the grass and pushing through it if it's tall. On dirt this means your coil is literally touching the dirt. Going slow means sweeping your coil much slower than normal, something in the order of four or five feet a second.

Keeping your coil low gives you the maximum depth your machine and coil can produce. Think about it; if your coil is one inch above the ground, that's one less inch of penetration into the ground you're getting.

Going slow gives your machine more time to separate out close targets. Today's processors are very fast, but going slow helps them perform even better. By going slow, a perceived single target in the ground may prove to be two targets. If one of those targets is a large nail, and the other is a silver dime, you might only detect the nail when moving fast. By scanning slower, you may detect the nail and the dime.

Both of these techniques will reduce the amount of ground you are able to cover in any given hunt, but they will both increase the likelihood that you'll find a good target if it's there. Remember, it's not how much ground you detect but how well you detect the ground.

Law enforcement

If you metal detect on public land, or even on private land in public view, you will be questioned by a law enforcement officer at some point in time, it's inevitable. This isn't a bad thing at all as they're most likely responding to a call from someone and it's an opportunity to introduce them to the hobby, and it just may lead to a new lead or permission for you.

When you see an officer pulling onto the property, or the officer approaching you, put your detector down, take your headphones off, and walk towards them with a smile on your face. This sends the subtle message that you have nothing to hide—because you don't.

On private land be sure to have the phone number of the owner with you if they are not home or not present at the land you are hunting. They won't be calling the police on you, but protective neighbors may be and a simple call can prove your legitimacy. Also be sure to have ID on you in case the owner doesn't answer the phone. The officer will want a record of whom they spoke with to prove they investigated the situation.

Much of the same is true of public land in how you address the officer and having ID on you but there are distinctive differences. The most obvious difference being that you're on public land so you don't need permission from anyone to be there. It's entirely possible that some curmudgeon called the police for any number of reasons or even an unscrupulous competitor who doesn't want you working "my" park called the police to complain about you.

Assuming you've done your homework and you are sure that there are no ordinances or laws against detecting public land, you have nothing to worry about.

So, when you see an officer approaching, stop what you're doing, approach them, and say, "Hi," with a big smile on your face. I've never had a negative interaction with an officer while metal detecting and find they're very reasonable. Answer any questions they may have about what you're doing and tell them about the hobby. They may know of a good location in town for you to hunt.

Should you run across the Rambo cop whose ego is bigger than his brain, just pack up your stuff and leave as requested, it's just not worth the hassle; there are too many places to detect to get worried about any one.

On one occasion, a couple friends and I were detecting a farm we had permission to be at when a police car came up the driveway towards us. The owner did not live on the property and, since we had spoken with the renters, we knew it wasn't the owner or resident who had called them. Seeing the car coming up the long driveway, I took off my headphones, put my gear down and walked towards the officer with a smile on my face.

As the officer got out of the car I said, "Nosey neighbors, huh?" and he stated that someone had called to report people trespassing on the land. I assured him that we were there with the permission of the owner, who happens to be a retired Boston professional athlete, and he could call him if he liked. The officer was surprised to learn who owned the property but did not want to bother him. He simply asked if I had identification, which I did, and he recorded who I was in case my story was a ruse, which it wasn't. No big deal.

Another time, my buddy Ron got us permission to hunt an old church on a main road in the town he lives in. When we arrived, I asked him, "How long do you figure before the cops show up?" And we both laughed. To our surprise, it took nearly two hours for a cruiser to arrive and nobody had called, the officer just happened to be driving by and was curious. He pulled up and asked, "Are you supposed to be doing that?" We told him that Father so and so had given us permission and, yes, we were supposed to be there. He asked a few questions about the hobby and went on his way without getting out of his car or checking our IDs.

There have been a few other instances where I've interacted with law enforcement while out detecting and they all went the same. I've never been asked to leave a public or private location by the police as I always have permission on private land and it's not illegal on public land in most locations. Keep this in mind; keep a positive attitude and a smile on your face and you shouldn't have any issues.

Legal issues

Disclaimer: I am not an attorney. All information is based on my experience, research, and lay understanding of the law as it pertains to where I reside and is for general information only. If you have any questions about legal issues, contact an attorney.

There are a number of legal issues as they pertain to metal detecting. Let's start with private property. If you are on someone's property without their permission you are trespassing and committing a crime. It's that simple, so don't do it. If you are trespassing on someone's property and removing items from the ground, you're stealing as well. Anything on or under the ground belongs to the landowner, period.

Private Property

In my experience, the landowner almost never has any interest in what you find. Some will want to see your finds simply out of curiosity.

There are some detectorists who offer to split or share finds with the landowner and, while it isn't the worst thing I've ever heard of, I generally don't do that myself. There are exceptions though; I tell landowners that if they have lost anything personal in their yard, I'll be happy to return it to them should I find it. I'll also return anything personally identifiable such as a class or wedding ring. I'm also primarily interested in coins so I don't mind handing over a relic or two out of goodwill rather than as a condition of permission. If a landowner insists on keeping whatever I find, I thank them for their time and move along. There are literally an endless supply of properties to search so skipping any one isn't a big deal.

Public Land

Anything that has ever been lost legally belongs to the owner—or their heirs—unless it was willfully abandoned.

With almost everything you'll find, you'll never be able to locate the rightful owner and it's effectively yours. If you find a class ring, the owner can be found; start by calling the high school the ring is from and ask for the librarian, they likely have every yearbook and might be able to ID the owner quickly. Or if you find a wedding band with an inscription on it you might be able to find the owner. In the case of a wedding band, I'd suggest putting a post in the lost and found section of Craigslist or your local paper describing the location of the find and a very general description of the ring such as "men's wedding band." If someone can tell you the inscription, then it's most likely theirs. Returning it brings a lot of goodwill to you and the hobby and it just feels great to help someone out.

I once found a military dog tag in the yard of an old house and the owner knew where the previous owner lived. The dog tag belonged to the previous owner's deceased husband and she was happy to have it. And it felt great to return this item.

Keep in mind that, legally speaking, all that lost change in the ground still belongs to whomever lost it. But how in the world would anyone ever determine who owns it? What did you do the last time you found a $5 bill lying on the ground? Did you try to find the rightful owner? I'll bet you kept it. Lost change is no different.

A note about willful abandonment.

If someone intentionally chooses to leave something behind, they have given up legal control of it. When you put your trash on the sidewalk, for example, you've willfully abandoned that property and anyone can take it.

Someone once told me a story about a friend of theirs being at a local waterfront hotspot and in a fit of rage at her fiancé she took off her engagement ring and threw it into the water. She willfully abandoned it, and
the ring would belong to whoever finds it. Now, if I knew how to scuba dive and had an underwater machine you can bet you know where I could go!

Federal Land

It is illegal to metal detect on federal land, especially parks. Don't do it. There are some exceptions I believe when it comes to Bureau of Land Management land out west, and with gold prospecting, but do your own research on that. Being in Rhode Island, I have no experience with BLM land.

The federal government follows the below listed acts among others:

1906 American Antiquities Act
1966 National Historic Preservation Act, amended 2000
1979 Archaeological Resources Act
1990 Native American Graves Protection and Repatriation Act

All of the above acts are designed to protect historical sites, graves, and Native American artifacts. They are intended to protect national treasures. They can and have been used to prosecute metal detectorists or bottle diggers who recover items on federal land so just don't do it. The Feds have no sense of humor at all when it comes to these regulations and if you're caught detecting on federal land, you'll be lucky to only have your equipment confiscated and be charged with trespassing. It could be worse.

Technically speaking, anything over 100 years old falls under the American Antiquities Act. This includes that 1912 wheat penny you dug on your last hunt. Now whom would you turn that wheat penny over to? The state archaeologist? The town/city government? The local historical society? The Federal Reserve? Use your common sense. It's very unlikely that the Feds want their 1912 wheat penny back; if they did there would be a lot of coin shops out of business.

State Land

Anything on or under state land belongs to the state. This doesn't mean you can't detect on state land, but you need to know the law in your state.

In my home state, it is illegal to metal detect on state owned land, thus I don't. I'm sure others have, but it's just not worth the slim chance of getting caught and being prosecuted, maybe even having your equipment confiscated.

State parks are a little different.

Detecting is allowed in "designated areas only" within the state park system, but it varies from park to park. This usually but not always refers to the beaches only. I know of some parks that allow detecting anywhere, the rangers just wave and drive on by. Other parks enforce the regulations to the nth degree.

A fair number of parks do not have rangers stationed on them at all, so I don't know who is going to tell you where the "designated area" is. I've hunted these types of parks without concern. Regardless of where you are, do you homework and know the law before you go. It could save you a big headache. And don't call city hall!

Coin cleaning

Cleaning coins can be a controversial subject in the field of metal detecting but much less so in numismatics where it's considered a crime against humanity. To make the purists and numismatists happy, let me state this first: don't clean your coins, period.

Why not clean your coins? Because by "cleaning" a coin you can very easily take a coin worth thousands and make it worth next to nothing. For this reason, I highly recommend that you *do not* clean coins in the field.

Resist the urge to wipe the dirt off of a coin because you will scratch the coin to some degree. And if it's a silver coin, you could scratch it a lot. Should you have the good fortune to find a rare coin, you don't want to devalue it. The chances of finding a rare and valuable coin are slim, but it happens. Search YouTube for "Dr. Tones 1901s" for a great example.

For the record, I don't clean my coins in the field; it's just not worth it. Though it's unlikely I'll ever find a coin like Dr. Tones' 1901s Barber quarter, why take the chance? Any silver coins I recover are simply wrapped in tissue paper and placed inside an Altoids tin in my pouch to check out later. I don't waste time cleaning coins in the field because not only can you damage them by "checking the date", but you're giving up valuable detecting time as well.

Cleaning Clad Coins

Since 1965, U.S. dimes and quarters have been clad coins. This means they have a copper core with an outer layer of silver-colored nickel-copper. The same is true of half dollars since 1970. When it comes to clad coins, I put them in a rock tumbler with some water and vinegar and let them bounce off of each other for a couple of hours to knock the dirt off before rolling them up and heading to the bank. They're only clad so it doesn't matter if they get scratched. Be sure to tumble pennies by themselves, and nickels by themselves, but dimes and quarters can go together.

In the case of nickels, be they Buffalos, Liberty Heads, or even Shield nickels, there really is only one way to clean them that works well. The purists will cringe, but I work them lightly with an SOS pad until enough detail emerges that I'm happy with them. Does this scratch the coin? Yes, yes it will. Does it destroy the coin? Nickels tarnish so badly in the ground that they're all worthless from a numismatic point of view, so why not at least be able to see what they are?

Cleaning Dug Silver Coins

When a silver coin comes out of the ground, it is treated differently. Silver gets special treatment because it is so soft that it *will scratch* simply by trying to pull or swipe any dirt off of it. Just wrap it in tissue and put it in a protective container.

To clean silver coins they're first soaked in warm water to loosen the dirt, this could take hours. I'll then hold a coin under running water to take more dirt off of it and/or hit it with the sink sprayer. At this point the coin can almost always be identified to determine if it is a key date or not. Usually this isn't the case and, since I like my silver to shine, it'll get cleaned with a little paste of baking soda rubbed between my thumb and forefinger and it cleans up very nicely almost all the time.

Beach Silver Coins

Silver coins that have come from the beach are another situation altogether. I don't worry about ruining them because they're always already ruined. They turn black in the ocean and that stuff does not want to come off. Sometimes they come with concretions attached.

To clean these, I heat a small glass bowl in the microwave to just below boiling. The coins are then wrapped in aluminum foil (shiny side towards the coin) and dropped in the water before adding a teaspoon of baking soda. It will bubble and hiss for several minutes and smell like sulfur. Once the bubbling stops most of the black crud will come off when rubbed under water. You may need to hit it with the baking soda paste to get the gunk off and if it is stubborn repeat the process from the beginning. This is a chemical cleaning and if done too aggressively—as I've done— can wipe away all of the details of a coin. It takes a little practice but works well.

If for some reason you think you have a valuable silver coin from the beach there is another much slower but effective method. I've done this a few times with beach silver coins when the crud was just too stubborn.

Place the coin in a shallow plastic bowl with just enough water to cover it and place in the freezer until solid. The less water the better as it freezes faster. Remove the bowl from the freezer and pour hot water on it. Some of the water will have penetrated the gunk and frozen and the rapid expansion when the coin gets hit with the hot water pops the junk off. You'll be able to see small pieces of dirt in the water after doing this. Be prepared to do this many times over to get the gunk off. It doesn't harm the coin and works well but takes a long time.

Another option is to soak the coin in olive oil. Olive oil is mildly acidic but does not damage the coin. Over time, it can loosen the junk that'll fall off when you hit it with the sink sprayer. The downside to this is that it can take a very long time. I generally put a coin in olive oil for a month, hit it with the sprayer, assess it, and usually put it back in the oil for another month and repeat until I've reached a level of cleanliness I'm comfortable with.

A more aggressive approach is to use Coca-Cola. It's more acidic than the olive oil and works a little faster. Soak a coin overnight then assess. For reasons unknown to me, Cherry Coke is the most acidic so make use of that info however you choose.

Cleaning Copper Coins

Be they wheat pennies, Indian Head pennies, large cents, or Colonial coppers they all pretty much clean up the same.

The first step is to take a toothpick and scrape off the loose dirt. This won't hurt the coin as the copper is tougher than the toothpick or the dirt really. Then take a firm toothbrush and brush the coin, you should be able to get most of the dirt off of it this way. Lastly, take a toothpick and pick the dirt out of all the letters, numbers, and crevices. The coin may still be dull and hard to see the details, but it will be clean. I've yet to use Andre's Pencils to clean copper coins but I have seen some fantastic results from using them so you may want to experiment with them using some dug copper pennies. You could also try the freezing and heating method if you want to be extra careful and have plenty of time on your hands.

Another option is to soak the coin in hydrogen peroxide. This will turn the coin a deep brown, but it will also get the dirt off. Soak the coin for a few hours, and then check it for dirt. If need be, scrub it with a cotton swab and soak more. Repeat until you've reached your desired level of cleanliness.

After cleaning, some people like to then rub paraffin wax on the coin and buff it with a soft cloth. Don't do this if you have a rare or valuable coin, but for your average Indian Head penny or large cent this makes it look pretty good. I prefer Renaissance wax, which is used by museums to protect delicate artifacts from environmental damage.

Cleaning other finds

There are a number of ways to clean your finds from the mildest to the most aggressive. Let's take a look at them from the least aggressive to the most.

Distilled Water: The simplest and least destructive way to clean your finds is to give them a soak in distilled water and let the water work on the dirt. I wouldn't do this for iron or steel objects as it'll be a catalyst for rust, but it works for mild dirt on all other metals.

Sonic Cleaners: These are jewelry cleaners that work great for mildly soiled items. Use either distilled water or filtered tap water in your cleaner and let it buzz away for several minutes. Much of the dirt will fall off, and some will be merely loosened. This is good for everything other than iron and steel.

Olive Oil: Olive oil is probably the most used cleaning method as it is mildly acidic but still very gentle and can be used on any metal. Simply put your item in a plastic container and cover in olive oil. Depending on the amount of buildup on your find, this could take days to months, but it is gentle and effective on all metals.

Vinegar: A 50/50 solution of white vinegar and water is a great cleaning agent; it's especially good for getting the junk off of clad coins. Just put a bunch of them in a plastic jar, cover with the solution, and shake away for a few minutes. Conversely, I've heard of people putting said jar of coins in the trunk of their car and letting them roll around for a few days to knock the dirt off. It works on most metals.

Coca-Cola: This stuff is more acidic than olive oil. But people do use it as a soak to get stubborn dirt and other contaminants off of finds. I remember as a child in the 1970s seeing my uncles use Coke to clean grease off of car parts and rust off of the body. Obviously, this works with all metals, but I would keep a somewhat close eye on badly corroded items as you might not want to remove all of the corrosion.

Electrolysis: This is the most aggressive form of cleaning and one I have yet to try; remember, I'm not a techie and electricity isn't something I like to play with. It is especially good at removing corrosion from iron items, though, and it is also used for silver and gold. Electrolysis needs close monitoring as it quite literally removes the surface of the metallic items. This approach takes skill and close observation to use. Make sure you know what you're doing before attempting this with anything potentially valuable.

Preserving your finds

Once you've made a good find or two, you may wish to put them on display, and some of them will need protection from the environment.

For cleaned iron items, a spray shellac is the most common way to preserve an item. It seals out the environment and prevents moisture from causing rusting. It's really the only way I know of that works.

With coins, you have a few choices depending on your personal taste and the metallic makeup of the coin.

There are all kinds of display options offered by various vendors. These all work well for silver coins or nickels. Copper coins can be a little different. For copper coins, I recommend Renaissance wax; it's what museums use for preserving artifacts and creating an environmental barrier. Some detectorists use paraffin wax as well. In both cases, apply the wax with a soft cloth and buff off any extra wax before storing or presenting your coin.

Once your finds are preserved, you can store them away or display them in whatever fashion you wish. Some use display cases, shadow boxes, or coin holders. It's up to you how you would like to display your items.

There's nothing good left

The first handheld metal detectors, known as the "metalascope", were produced by Fisher Labs in 1931, though they were primarily used by the military for mine detection. With the invention of the transistor in 1947, metal detectors began to get smaller and more practical. In 1964, Charles Garrett changed the industry by solving the problem of oscillator drift making handheld metal detectors truly a functional and handheld machine.

Since then, countless people have been searching for and recovering all kinds of amazing items with their metal detectors. This might make you think that "there's nothing good left" if people have been vacuuming up good finds for over fifty years, but it's just not true.

Let's consider the humble American dime, for example.

Very few silver dimes, practically none, have been lost since 1964. But that doesn't mean that a lot of them aren't still out there just waiting for you to find them. Let's take a look at how many silver dimes were minted in the first place.

Draped Bust Dimes	1796–1806:	11,710,194 minted
Capped Bust Dimes	1809–1837:	13,058,700 minted
Liberty Seated Dimes	1837–1891:	247,477,444 minted
Barber Dimes	1892–1916:	504,509,041 minted
Winged Liberty Dimes	1916–1945:	2,173,857,800 minted
Roosevelt Dimes	1945–1964:	5,163,190,360 minted

In total, over 8.1 *billion silver dimes* have been put into circulation by the U.S. Mint. "But wait," you say, "lots of them were melted down when silver went over $100 an ounce in February of 1980." You are right. But none of the coins that were in the ground in 1980 got melted down; they had been lost and couldn't be melted. Now, if we assume that a mere one percent of all dimes were lost, then we are talking about over 8,100,000 silver dimes getting lost, the vast majority of them in the ground. Using the three percent the U.S. Mint uses, we're talking nearly 25,000,000 dimes. In melt weight alone, at current prices, that is over 2.5 billion dollars' worth of silver. Let that sink in for a minute.

If we were to do the math for quarters, half dollars, and dollars, not to mention the rarer trade dollars, war nickels, three-cent silvers, and twenty-cent coins, we would be talking about tens of millions of coins. And there simply are not enough of us out there with detectors to have found all of those yet and won't be in your lifetime for sure. There are still so many silver coins out there that I consider any hunt that doesn't produce at least one silver coin to be a disappointment, and I'm not often disappointed.

Let's not forget that there are a lot of valuable things being lost every day. People still wear precious metals and stones as jewelry and they still lose them. Cell phones didn't exist in the past, but everyone has one now and people lose them. Cell phones, tablets, MP3 players and all kinds of electronic devices get lost daily and have value even in non-working condition. There is quite literally a never-ending supply of modern, valuable things being lost every day.

So don't get stuck thinking that there isn't anything good left out there, or there are no good places left to hunt, because it just isn't true. Silver, gold, electronics, and other valuables are out there waiting to be found. Go find them.

It's never hunted out

"It's hunted out."

You will hear this phrase a lot, especially in reference to public places.

We've all heard that story before, someone tells you that a place has been pounded for years and nothing is left or, better yet, *they* have found nothing there so there isn't anything to find. Don't believe them.

When I first started detecting, I asked a buddy of mine, who is a very experienced hunter, if he'd had any success at a certain beach. The beach in question saw a lot of activity from the 1890s to the 1960s and he told me that he had success in years past but that it was now "hunted out." Not knowing any better I took him at his word and didn't bother going there.

Fast forward a few years and I'd learned a lot more and one day went to the "hunted out" beach. When I arrived, there were ominous clouds nearby, but I decided to give it a go until or unless the rain drove me away.

Walking onto the beach, I turned on my detector and literally on the first swing of the detector a very solid and repeatable signal rang out. I reached down and brought up an 1899 Barber dime on the first swing of the coil! *Well, this is promising,* I thought. I started working towards a small, rocky cut in the beach and within a few minutes hit a Seated dime, an 1876 Carson City Mint, and, minutes later, another Barber dime, a 1902. Literally within ten minutes I had two Barbers and a Seated dime.

Things slowed down pretty quickly but didn't stop, and neither did the clouds. They were moving in closer, and off shore I could see lightning strikes. Over the course of the next forty-five minutes or so, I dug a small number of clad coins and a Mercury dime and just before the rain got bad enough to chase me off of the beach, I found another Seated dime. This one was too far worn to get a date off of but a Seated dime is a Seated dime, I'll never complain about the condition of one.

As you may imagine, I've been back to this beach many times and while no hunt has ever lived up to that first one it continues to produce Mercury and Barber dimes and the occasional Seated dime as well, not to mention lots of bottles and the occasional piece of jewelry and one Walking Liberty half dollar. A detectorist I know dug three half-real coins in one summer at this "hunted out" beach in 2016. My most recent venture there produced a small amount of clad, a Braided Hair large cent, a three-cent nickel, and an 1854 Seated Liberty dime.

When you hear a place is "hunted out," don't believe it for two reasons.

First, unless you're talking about a small yard, it's pretty much impossible to hunt any place clean. And, second, someone may be either mistaken or attempting to hide a good location from you. No location is ever hunted out until you decide that the targets are so few and far between that the location just isn't worth your time anymore.

But even then, it's still not hunted out.

White whales & bucket list items

It's entirely likely that even before starting in the hobby, you'll have a wish list of things you'd love to find someday. This is your bucket list. As you gain experience in the hobby, your bucket list may shrink or grow as you cross items off your wish list because you've found them and added new ones because you've learned of items you didn't know existed at all such as a particular variety of coin.

In time, you will likely develop a white whale. This is the item that, given the amount of time you have spent in the hobby, it defies logic that you haven't found an example of it yet. In my case it was a silver half dollar.

I had been serious about the hobby for over five years and had never found a silver half dollar. I had found gold jewelry, diamond jewelry, Barber coins, Liberty Seated coins, Spanish Reals, two-cent coins, three-cent coins, and all kinds of other items, but for some reason the silver half eluded me. Given the amount of time I had spent hunting, a silver half should have shown up under my coil but it didn't.

Finally, one day, I was hunting an old farmhouse with a friend and just outside of the back door there was a big, old shady tree. I started working the area around the tree as people surely sat there in the days before air conditioning. It was at this spot that my first Walking Liberty half dollar showed up.

The irony of the situation was that on my next hunt, just a few days later, I found another Walking Liberty half. It seemed like, once my white whale had been found, halves began to show up with some frequency as I got three that summer.

So when that bucket list item or white whale eludes you, don't get frustrated. Just keep detecting and it will happen for you eventually, some day.

Scrap Metal

Before ending this book, I'd like to mention the practice of scrapping metal.

Many detectorists, me included, keep a few five-gallon buckets in their garage or basement for scrap metal. You will recover a lot of it and you can simply throw it away or turn it into cash.

I keep a bucket in my garage for lead, copper, and brass respectfully. When one of them fills up, I take it to the local scrap yard and cash it in. This does a couple of things for me.

Firstly, it puts a few dollars in my pocket for gas money to go metal detecting.

Secondly, when it comes to lead, it removes this unhealthy metal from the environment. When sitting in the ground, lead leaches into the plants, gets into the food chain, and ultimately makes its way up to apex predators, humans. You'll find an enormous number of lead sinkers at beaches, and you'll be surprised by how much lead piping and lead flashing you'll find in yards. It isn't worth much, but cashing it in is a win-win for you and the environment.

One last thing before I wrap up the book. Always check your trash before throwing it out.

I always check my trash because I'm separating out lead, copper and brass and also because sometimes you mistake items in the field. I've pulled silver items out of my trash that got there because they looked like aluminum. I've found interesting finds in my trash because they were so encrusted that I didn't notice what they were in the field. And one time, I found a 14k gold ring with diamonds in my trash that I nearly threw away because I thought it was costume jewelry.

So, before sending your junk off to wherever it goes, take a minute to go through it piece by piece, you just might find something good in there.

Acknowledgements

I want to thank my wife for her encouragement in regards to this project. Without her, I'm not sure this book would have happened. She constantly encouraged me, and her advice has been of immeasurable value.

When I first got serious about this hobby, Scott Lannan was an experienced hobbyist who helped me learn about the hobby. He was generous both with his knowledge, and good places to go metal detecting. Without his help, my learning curve would certainly have been steeper. This book is in part my way of repaying Scott by helping others.

Ron Kozoil helped me elevate my skills to a new level. Ron is the most successful person I've ever known when it comes to getting permission to metal detect private properties. He credits his success to his "Polish charm." Ron inspired me to improve my "door knocking" skills and this has led to many a memorable find.

Lastly, I want to thank my editor Ken Darrow, M.A. He took my draft and gave it the fine polish it needed to be ready for print. His knowledge and attention to detail impressed me greatly, and I want to recognize his efforts.

This last page is the only one Ken never saw. If it does not live up the level Ken brought my previous writing to, please accept my apologies.

Brian Maloney
July 2019

www.detectinglife.com
Instagram: @DiggingRI